McGraw-Hill Reading WonderWorks

Unit 9
Decodable Reader

McGraw Hill Education

Bothell, WA • Chicago, IL • Columbus, OH • New York, NY

Contents

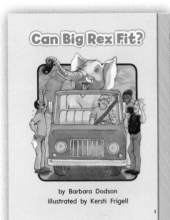

Get Set! Ride!

by Martin Rogowski
illustrated by Meryl Henderson

17

Can Big Rex Fit?

by Barbara Dodson

illustrated by Kersti Frigell

This is Big Rex.
Big Rex got big.
Big Rex got sick.

Can Big Rex fit in **here**?
It can get Rex to the vet.
What a big job!

4

Rex did not **want** to get in.
Big Rex dug in.
Big Rex did not go.

The men did not quit.
Rex did not get in.
Can **they** get him in?

Yes, we win.
Big Rex got in.
Big Rex did it!

Big Rex can fit.
The men nod to **me**.
I zip Big Rex to the vet.

Wake Up!

by Jacqueline Carter

illustrated by Laura Logan

Wake up, wake up!
Jane and Kate had a nap.

Jane and Kate gaze up.
Can they run in the sun?
It is not safe.

Kate can dig, dig, dig in.
Jane can **help** Kate dig in.
They can make a safe cave.

Jane and Kate wake up late.
The sun is not up yet.
Kate and Jane can gaze up.

Jane can see a big tan box.
Kate can see it, **too**.
Can Jane make a fun game?

Yes! Jane can hop up on it.
Hop, hop, hop on it, Kate.
Jane made up a fun game!

Get Set! Ride!

by Martin Rogowski

illustrated by Meryl Henderson

Jan and Ike like to **play**.
They can ride a bike.
Yes, Jan and Ike are quick.

Nine ride up, up, up.
Nine ride up the lane.
Jan can ride up.

Jan and Ike ride on.
Jan led Ike.
Jan gave Rex a quick nod.

The side lane is safe.
Jan and Ike ride in line.

Jan and Ike ride, ride, ride.
Can Ike get a quick time?
Can Jan win it?

Jan **has** a quick, quick time!
Ike did not quite win.
Jan and Ike had a fine ride!

Unit 9

Decodable Words

Target Phonics Elements: Review Short *u*;
Consonants /g/g, /ks/x, /v/v, /j/j, /qu/qu, /w/w, /y/y, /z/z

big, dig, dug, got, get, job, Rex, quit, vet, win, yes, zip
Review: *can, did, fat, fit, him, in, it, men, nod, not, sick*

High-Frequency Words

here, me, they, this, want, what,
Review: *a, go, is, the, to, we*

Decodable Words

Target Phonics Element: Long *a* (*a_e*)

cave, game, gaze, Jane, Kate, late, made, make, safe, wake
Review: *big, box, can, dig, fun, had, hop, in, it, nap, not, on, run, sun, tan, up, yes, yet*

High-Frequency Words

help, too
Review: *a, and, is, see, the, they*

Week 3 • *Get Set! Ride!*

Word Count: 93

Decodable Words
Target Phonics Element: Long *i* (*i_e*)
bike, fine, Ike, lane, like, line, nine, quite, ride, side, time
Review: *can, gave, get, had, in, it, Jan, lane, led, nod, not, on, quick, Rex, safe, set, up, win, yes*

High-Frequency Words
has, play
Review: *a, and, are, is, the, they, to*

Decoding skills taught to date:

Consonants /m/*m*, /s/*s*, /p/*p*, /t/*t*; Short *a*; Short *i*; Initial and Final /n/*n*; Initial /k/*c*; Short *o*; Initial and Final /d/*d*; Consonant /h/*h*; Short *e*; Consonants /f/*f*, /r/*r*; Initial and Final /b/*b*; Consonant /l/*l*; Initial /k/*k*; Digraph *ck*; Short *u*; Initial and Final /g/*g*; Consonant /w/*w*; Consonants /ks/*x*, /v/*v*; Consonants /j/*j*, /qu/*qu*; Consonants /y/*y*, /z/*z*; Long *a* (*a_e*); Long *i* (*i_e*)